Shawna's Outreach:

When we each give a little,
a lot gets done

by

Shawna Thibodeau
and Amanda Sterczyk

Thibodeau, Shawna and Sterczyk, Amanda, authors
Shawna's Outreach: When we each give a little, a lot gets done

Issued in print and electronic formats.

ISBN: 9798393888824

1. Homelessness 2. Homeless outreach 3. Poverty
4. Sociology of urban areas 5. Social issues

Editor: Jennifer Rae-Brown, Christie Phillips
Cover: image Jonathan West, design TS
Layout: Matthew Bin
Published by Kindle Direct Publishing

Land Acknowledgement

This book was created on the traditional and unceded Algonquin Anishinaabe territory. Algonquin people lived in the Ottawa Valley for at least 8,000 years before the arrival of Europeans in North America, and they are the customary keepers and defenders of the Ottawa River Watershed and its tributaries. From coast to coast to coast, we respectfully acknowledge the ancestral and unceded territory of all First Nations, Inuit, and Métis peoples who call this land home.

Shawna Thibodeau is a proud Mi'kmaw woman, hailing from Nova Scotia, traditional Mi'kmaw territory.

Dedication

Shawna's Dedication

**To Rob, George, Harlen,
Sam, and Calvin**

This book is dedicated to all our street
friends, some of whom became closer
friends and some of whom are no longer
with us.

Thank you to my dad,
for teaching me that I can figure out how to
do something about it.

Contents

Foreword

I first met Shawna Thibodeau at a local Ladies Who Lunch (LWL) networking event. It was the first that I had attended in many years; I was no longer a regular attendee, having shelved my own business and returned to the paid workforce for a number of years. But in 2023, newly retired, I was determined to spend more time promoting *my* books, instead of treating them like the side hustle which they had inevitably become.

It was Shawna's first time at an LWL event. She had been gifted a ticket and directed to show up at the National Arts Centre for the luncheon. Following the meal, Shawna, to her surprise, heard LWL Founder Catherine Landry invite her to stand up and make herself known. Next, the group learned of an incredible act of generosity: a local real estate firm was donating $1,000 to Shawna's grassroots initiative, *Shawna's Outreach*. Catherine then invited Shawna to the microphone so that she could shine a light on her work with homeless people in Ottawa.

What followed was an impromptu speech by Shawna. Speaking from the heart, she explained how her work is a means of giving comfort to people living on the street, so that they know someone cares about them and that they have not been forgotten. In addition to providing food and other tangibles, Shawna is providing hope to people whose circumstances often lead to hopelessness.

By the time Shawna returned to her seat, there were few dry eyes in the room. But Catherine was not yet through supporting *Shawna's Outreach*. Each table was then asked to come up with a way in which they could help Shawna in her mission. Over the course of the afternoon, many women wandered over to speak with Shawna and chat about how they could contribute to her initiative.

I knew instantly that my support would involve writing. As an international author, I was, at that time, working on the manuscript for my twelfth book. I approached Shawna and pitched the idea of a book about *Shawna's Outreach*. It could help raise funds and awareness, with all royalties being directed to her work. In essence, I volunteered my time and services to write the book, and also committed to finding an editorial team that would also donate their services for free.

Shawna tells as many people as will listen: "When we each give a little, a lot gets done." This book is my way of giving a little so that a lot gets done.

Amanda Sterczyk
Co-author

Introduction

Millions of people around the world lack stable, safe, and secure housing, and the numbers keep rising. Many communities are grappling with a homelessness crisis. It is a complex dilemma with many interrelated factors, including but not limited to: a lack of affordable housing, a rising number of people facing mental health and substance use issues, growing poverty fueled by increasing inflation and workers' wages failing to keep pace, an increase in cases of domestic violence, racial and economic inequality, and a lack of affordable and accessible health care. Social programs struggle to provide adequate services to the growing number of people in need. Donations to charities dwindle as individuals feel the pinch of inflation in their wallets. Program funding is cut as governments try to do more with less. Combined, these factors stretch the social safety net beyond its capacity, and the system suffers ever-widening cracks.

These cracks allow people to fall through the safety net. But these cracks also bring about grassroots solutions that step in where established programs and organizations cannot. This, in essence, is what *Shawna's Outreach* has done. It serves to fill a gap, directly addressing the needs of homeless people in Ottawa. It also demonstrates how grassroots initiatives can collaborate effectively with established social programs—connecting the dots to close these gaps in government-provided assistance.

The primary aim of this book is to raise awareness of Ottawa's homeless crisis—adults and teens are being forced to eke out an existence in public spaces—and, at the same time, we want to show how small acts of kindness can accumulate into a groundswell of support for our most vulnerable neighbours. As Shawna points out to anyone who will listen, "If you do not know how to help, you will not help. If you see others helping out, you will be more inclined to help in whatever way you can."

Shawna's Outreach strives to bring hope to the homeless for 'One More Day.' Our hope is that readers from all walks of life will understand that homeless people are, first and foremost, people.

Note: Identifying information about individuals and organizations has been modified or omitted. This step ensures that people's confidences are maintained.

Disclaimer: The experiences described are Shawna's alone, and they may differ from those of other people.

Chapter One:
Backstory

Who is Shawna?

Originally from Atlantic Canada, Shawna is no stranger to the shelter system. She is a survivor of abuse, but that's a story for another time.[1] Shawna and her child stayed in a shelter for abused women and children in Nova Scotia in 2008; "for their own safety" was the recommendation from local law enforcement at the time.

While in the shelter for the first time, Shawna received a shower caddy filled with toiletries and personal hygiene products. Providing these items to residents of women's shelters is an essential part of creating a safe, supportive, and empowering environment for women who have experienced domestic violence, homelessness, or other challenging circumstances. While it helps women keep clean and prevents the spread of germs and infections, it also allows them to maintain their dignity and well-being. When women are going through difficult times, having access to such items can contribute to their sense of self-worth. This type of support is also practical, as many women arrive at a shelter with limited personal belongings, particularly if they have

---

[1]. Shawna is collaborating on a book about her personal history, to be published in the future.

left their homes abruptly to escape a dangerous or abusive situation.

Shawna moved from Meteghan, Nova Scotia, to Ottawa in 2008. Once she was able to secure a place of her own, she began searching local give-away groups online to find free furniture and household items. That's how she learned of Project Purse and Tanya O'Connor's efforts to collect toiletries and personal hygiene products for women experiencing homelessness in the Ottawa area. Shawna reached out to Tanya, letting her know that while time was all that she could offer, she wanted to support her cause in whatever way she could.

Shawna's spirit of giving and helping others continued, as she also supported Tanya's other initiatives, known as Tampon Tuesday Ottawa and Project Winter Warmth Ottawa. Tampon Tuesday saw people donate menstrual products, which, despite being among the most requested items at local food banks and shelters, are the least donated. Project Winter Warmth had people gathering items to stave off the cold for the less fortunate.

In addition to being a Maritimer, Shawna's heritage includes Mi'kmaw and Acadian roots. While each community is unique, members of all three share many traits, including resiliency, a sense of community, and a love of storytelling. In

Shawna's eyes, the other homeless women she met, whether they were in the shelter system or living on the street, were just like her. She saw them as her community, and she knew she needed to help. She began by collecting items that people were giving away and bringing them to shelters, but that was just the beginning.

While in Nova Scotia, Shawna had embarked on a Bachelor of Education at Université Saint-Anne, and went on to complete a diploma in Educational Software Development at Collège d'Acadie. She had also volunteered in schools in Nova Scotia, in positions ranging from teacher's aide to language monitor.

After moving to Ottawa, and despite her educational accomplishments, several compounding factors meant that Shawna was unable to work full-time: she was living with an anxiety disorder, had been diagnosed with post-traumatic stress disorder (PTSD) following the abuse she had endured, and was involved in multiple in-progress court cases that demanded her time and focus. In addition, as a welfare recipient, she was not allowed to work full-time but rather was required to complete volunteer hours in lieu of paid employment. With her background in education, she began by volunteering at her child's elementary school. Recognizing their need for extra help, she offered her time, in particular, to teachers of split classes. Over the years, Shawna stepped up to volunteer wherever help was needed, and even helped teach English to young newcomers.

Having initially been on welfare and then in the Ontario Disability Support Program (ODSP), Shawna had been given links to numerous organizations that help people in need, which set her on her volunteering journey within the capital city. She felt that having had her own struggles with mental health gave her a better understanding of the issues facing people on the street. She was happy to donate her time and energy to help others less fortunate than herself: "Volunteering was my way of giving back and feeling like I was earning my money."

How Did Shawna's Outreach Begin?

Shawna began donating clothes to shelters in Ottawa in 2010: "I always questioned people dropping clothes into a donation box when there was such a need elsewhere. I borrowed a friend's car to deliver loads of clothes, alternating between shelters and drop-ins."

In 2018, Shawna began dedicating her volunteer time to support an established grassroots initiative, where she was eventually named Director of Outreach. This organization provided assistance to unhoused people and those living in poverty in Ottawa. Shawna's role included monthly, or sometimes bimonthly, outreach walks. Outreach involves finding vulnerable people wherever they are living on the street and offering them the support that they may need. This help can include first aid, mental health support, or direction to essential services. Outreach workers can also carry supplies such as blankets, clothing, and food with them, to distribute as needed.

A key component of successful outreach is relationship-building, as homeless people need to trust the individuals who are offering to help them survive and—ultimately—to thrive, as they work toward their transition from life on the street.

Beyond her role as Director of Outreach, Shawna also completed her own city walks. She took it upon herself to meet others involved in delivering outreach services and people working in shelters, to determine how they could work together to best support those in need. As an example of "the whole being greater than the sum of its parts," Shawna was struck by the potential economies of scale: if the various groups were able to combine their efforts, their impact on the unhoused population would be all the greater. She also saw combining their support as a way to distribute items more effectively and share more widely, as well as raise awareness of each group's mission by sharing social media content.

On the outreach walks, Shawna and other volunteers pulled a wagon overflowing with needed supplies. These included: in winter, an insulated urn for hot food contributed by restaurants or individuals; and in summer, sandwiches or other foods, and drinks, that had been donated. Other types of donations—outerwear, undergarments, condoms, first aid supplies, etc.—were also loaded into the wagon for distribution. Before long, those on the streets began to recognize the wagon and would hurry to see what might be available. They understood the people associated with it to be their allies, and felt comfortable asking for items that would meet their most basic needs.

These outreach walks were entirely volunteer driven and initiated. Shawna posted the walk schedule through social media, and anyone could sign up to participate. The group would meet at a central location—often, Ottawa City Hall—and split into two subgroups to cover as much of the downtown core as possible. New volunteers often commented, after taking part or during the walks, how they were shocked to discover that homeless people are just like everyone else. Homeless people are kind.

Homeless people don't simply take everything. Homeless people aren't constantly on drugs. Most importantly, new volunteers came to realize that the situation on the street is far worse than people know, and that the access we assume is out there is complicated by many barriers.

In March 2020, when COVID-19 was declared a global pandemic, everything changed for unhoused people and those providing support to them. Public health restrictions had a dire impact on many outreach organizations, and on the people they were serving. Government-funded outreach workers, for example, were pulled off the street. In February 2021, the ongoing pandemic forced closure of the organization where Shawna had been volunteering as an outreach leader.

While she was compelled to give up that position, Shawna realized that she could not stop reaching out to those on the street. The need for outreach services grew more acute as donations of all kinds dropped. Ottawa faced considerable job losses during pandemic lockdowns, which meant people were less charitable towards vulnerable populations. And while gift cards for restaurants seemed a good idea for homeless individuals, closures meant they were not able to redeem them. Once they reopened, many restaurants initially took only drive-through orders, which proved a challenge for un-housed people without access to a vehicle.

Panhandlers on the street could no longer rely on a steady stream of downtown workers sharing their spare change. Those asking for change at traffic lights had barely any donations, as fewer people were driving to work. The people who lived on the street had no access to washrooms once businesses and public spaces shut down.

By this time, Shawna had already spent several years in street outreach. She recognized that she would have to do whatever she could with the support of the grocery stores, food banks, restaurants, and individuals who could still afford to donate food and other items. In many cases, those donating doubled what they had been giving, and Shawna headed out to distribute whatever she received. Shelters had closed temporarily and were not accepting new clients. It was a scary time for those already in shelters and for those living on the street, with less support available since outreach workers had been instructed to cease work. Because Shawna had worked strictly as a volunteer and was not registered as an employee, "As Shawna" she was able to check on friends on the street and bring whatever she had to those in need: "I could bring water; I could bring snacks; I could bring toilet paper."

Shawna's Outreach was born in February 2021. It began with a Facebook page, sharing photos of donated items and stories of Shawna's experiences distributing these donations on the street, to raise awareness of Ottawa's homeless crisis and draw in more donations. From its beginnings, Shawna has received no payment for her work, and *Shawna's Outreach* is still not funded.

Through her commitment over the past decade, Shawna has met hundreds of people from all walks of life. She says, "Everyone has something to give. One person has a bar of soap, another person has shampoo, and another person has five minutes of time to share a post on Facebook. It's whatever we can give. That's what I do: I take these items and I walk the streets. But most of all, I am Mi'kmaq, I am French Acadian, I am a Maritimer, so I can do this [Shawna makes the sign of a hand puppet, a gesture that indicates she can yarn—aka talk and tell stories]. I sit beside people on the street and I let them tell me their stories, whether it's about their last puff on a crack pipe or the fact that they haven't eaten in three days, or that they had to sell their bodies to have a safe place to sleep in a parking garage in Ottawa. Whatever it is they want to tell me, I sit with them and I talk about it. But

I have also developed an 'outreach bag' after many years of these stories. And in that bag are items that get them through 'One More Day'. Tomorrow might be the day their family finds them. Tomorrow might be the day they get housing. Tomorrow might be the day they get accepted to rehab. The system is messy; we're all working our hardest to help. Can I fix the system? Nope. Can I feed someone? Damn straight I can, so that's what I do. Every penny I get helps someone in need."

Humanizing Outreach

At its core, *Shawna's Outreach* is a labour of love. Shawna works tirelessly to help those in need. She is on the streets several times per month, helping our most vulnerable neighbours. Shawna's goal with all of her outreach work is to recognize and value the people she encounters—to humanize them, if you will.

Shawna has helped deliver countless items of a practical nature to unhoused people, but just as important are the many intangibles she shares with them. To all those she meets, Shawna offers dignity, respect, and conversation without judgement. She has also volunteered with other organizations that help homeless people in other ways. One, for example, offers free haircuts. Here, Shawna recalls witnessing the moment of dignity the act can afford the recipient—a parent feeling confident about going to their child's wedding, or a mother being excited to have their photograph taken with their child. And at Odawa Friendship Centre, an Indigenous drop-in centre for First Nations, Inuit, and Métis families, Shawna has even dressed up as Santa Claus. She does not see a person's religion, their colour, or their clothing. She simply wants everyone to be okay and helps whenever she can.

Shawna is dedicated to providing impartial support to the unhoused population. As a result, she is seen as a trusted individual. In one case, a panhandler asked Shawna to hold the can he used for collecting money—a significant gesture when we consider how theft is a constant threat for those living on the street. In another case, Shawna picked up and delivered prescription medication to a homeless person. On a regular basis, she walked the downtown streets until she located him, then watched him smile as he let her know how much better he felt, the moment he had swallowed his medication.

Shawna is as committed to sharing content for this book as she is to supporting unhoused people: "I don't want to miss anything because everybody is so important. I go to bed at night and ideas cross my mind about things that should be in this book—important things that have happened, stories I have experienced. I'm concerned that once we finish this book, I'll remember some good ones. These stories are important; they are learning experiences and a reminder that these people matter. Many of them are no longer with us, but their lessons will live on through this book and through my social media posts. My experiences with homeless people are my way of giving my little bit to make a big difference. I use my time; I collect items; I prepare them."

Shawna describes the situation in this way, "There is no food, no coupon, no donation I can't find a home for. I have delivered thousands of street outreach bags into the hands of people in need."

Chapter Two:
Do Good

A Day in the Life of *Shawna's Out-reach*

What does a "typical" day in the life of *Shawna's Outreach* look like? From Shawna's stories, we learn that while there are no typical days, the one constant is that she fills every hour.

Nothing is planned, nor can it be antici-pated, as far as donations and calls for help go. And yet, almost daily, Shawna gets at least one message from someone offering something: a case of water, shoes they no longer wear, etc. And several times per month, she also receives messages asking for help: "Hi, I've been to the food bank, but I don't have enough snacks for my kids," or "Hey Shawna, my boyfriend and I just got our first place, but we can't afford food."

So many people reach out to Shawna asking for help, but thankfully, a greater number of people get in touch offering do-nations, which she can then redistribute. In another example of support that goes be-yond tangible, she now has a number of in-dividuals and businesses around Ottawa that offer up their premises as designated drop-off locations, where donations can be left. Before this, it required Shawna to drive around the city to collect donations. While she still needs to visit these self-designated drop-offs (and always within their opening hours), some individuals who gather donations for her outreach will bring them to her home. Small acts of kindness like these allow Shawna to spend more time delivering donations.

Shawna makes every effort to plan donation pick-ups to maximize her use of gas and time, yet she can never know when a business, food bank, or shelter will call to say they have a donation ready for her. Sometimes the size of a donation that they want to pass on can add another layer of complexity to her day. Here are some examples of generous—but last-minute—donations:

- 13,000 lollipops
- 1,800 eggs
- 200 meal prep/food delivery boxes (refused by some Ottawa residents during the early days of the pandemic, when it was feared that the virus could be spread through touching infected surfaces).

Donations like these need to be redistributed quickly to preserve food that would otherwise need refrigerating.

Inevitably, every day in *Shawna's Outreach* also includes much sorting. Donations arrive in varying states of packaging and need to be triaged based on their final destination. Depending on what Shawna receives and how it can best be utilized, she will sometimes pass items on to other organizations who help vulnerable citizens. Several times a week, Shawna sorts donations and sends emails about redirecting some of them elsewhere. She has a shelf in the back room (of her very small condo!) that is designated for street outreach. While Shawna used to accept all clothing donations, she now limits her street outreach to winter wear, small blankets, and select undergarments: "Your home can quickly get overwhelmed with clothing. Add to that the risks of bedbugs, lice, and mould if they are sitting in your home." Damaged clothing can be a particular challenge; while there were groups that in the past would repurpose them for use, it's now harder to find a home for such items.

Unfortunately, some people don't take sufficient care to ensure that their donations are of usable quality or that they are safely packaged. Items like these pose a risk to personal health and safety, and yet they have been included in donations Shawna has received, including broken glass, cement blocks, cat feces, chewed or broken items, mouse droppings, and mouldy clothing.

Let Me Bend Your Ear

Anyone who loves a good story will tell you that storytelling is a two-way street. Great storytellers are also great listeners, as they want to hear our stories as much as they want to share their own. Shawna, being a natural storyteller due to her heritage, is great on both fronts: she shares her stories, but she also listens to others' stories with openness and authenticity.

When Shawna is delivering outreach supplies to panhandlers on the street, she will sit and talk with them. She listens to discover the motivation behind their panning. Some are simply trying to make enough money to pay for their next meal, while others will spend a week panning so they can afford to stay in a hotel for a night. As well as giving security, a hotel room offers a shower and the chance to sleep in a comfortable bed, instead of on the hard pavement. Shawna has learned of people trying to raise money for bus fare or for their child's school lunch. Often, these conversations are a homeless person's way of explaining how and why they ended up on the street. Regardless of why they are panning, Shawna helps where she can.

Shawna has heard about many roads that have led to homelessness. Each story is heartbreaking in its own way. Unique to

each individual, the stories do, nevertheless, echo a theme on circumstances that
have led to their becoming homeless. Many
of them:

- were not accepted for who they are;
- have suffered abuse;
- face mental health challenges; or
- are dealing with trauma stem-
  ming from any of the above.

Shawna believes in listening because
"These stories are important; they are learning experiences and a reminder that these
people matter." This is the reason behind
her sharing the story of her outreach work.
Shawna is regularly invited to make community presentations, for example, at every
level of schooling from preschool to college;
in businesses such as dental offices; and
even museums. People want to learn from
Shawna's Outreach to understand how they
can help. Shawna takes every opportunity
she can to speak about the needs of unhoused people and those on a low-income.

On one occasion, a high school English
teacher invited Shawna into her class to tell
the group about her life story. But the inter-
action went much further. The students
joined Shawna in an outreach walk, helping
her to distribute outreach bags and talking
to the recipients. The students were then
tasked with—in place of writing an English

essay—creating a 10-minute video presentation on an aspect of homelessness.

Another speaking engagement led to students from Revel Academy (a small, private school in Ottawa) making weekly meals to share with High Jinx, a neighbourhood support organization. The group had not heard of this community hub in central Ottawa until Shawna raised awareness about some of the organizations that help people in need.

Who Contributes to *Shawna's Outreach*?

The students Shawna meets through in-school presentations are often keen to contribute to *Shawna's Outreach*. Very often, the end of her presentation sees students approaching her as they reach into their pockets. They might present her with a coffee shop gift card, for example, or they may offer up their unopened, prepackaged food items that Shawna can then share with a homeless person.

Shawna receives weekly messages from people wanting to donate toiletries after a cull and reorganization of their bathroom. If she is given large containers, she uses them to fill travel size ones that can be donated to shelters, or places like High Jinx, for individual use.

While Shawna prefers to receive donations of food and goods, some people prefer to give her money. In these cases, she finds a way to stretch every dollar donated, taking advantage of sales to buy goods in multiples or purchasing restaurant gift cards in bulk.

In one instance, a lottery winner was keen to share their wealth by giving a sizeable donation to *Shawna's Outreach.* They had seen a social media post about Shawna's work and wanted to do their part. Shawna entrusted the donation to a friend while she compiled a wish list of essential goods, which she then purchased with this generous donation. To some, such a donation might be seen as "giving a lot," whereas the lottery winner likely viewed it as "giving a little," since they were sharing a small portion of an unexpected windfall. In Shawna's eyes, the move reinforces how powerful word of mouth can be—the lottery winner directed their donation to her grassroots initiative after hearing about it. Many of the donations directed to *Shawna's Outreach* are the result of her drive: being mentioned in a social media post or talked about among family, friends, or co-workers.

Shawna is grateful to all those who donate to or spread awareness of her initiative. In her mind, no act is too small. She doesn't like to refuse donations of any sort because she is keen to encourage the giving spirit. If she does not have use for an item, she will direct the donation to another organization that helps at-risk individuals.

The only items Shawna has ever refused are pianos. Yes, that's pianos—plural. She has been offered a piano on two occasions. In one case, the donation came with strings attached: the donor told Shawna that she could not sell the piano. Understandably, this posed a conundrum for her. While a piano can't be used for outreach, the cash from the sale of an item like this could fund many items on Shawna's outreach wish list. The logistics of a piano were another issue: Shawna had no interest in lifting it, carrying it, tuning it, or worrying about it, so in both cases, she responded with a polite, "No, thank you!"

What Do 13,000 Lollipops Look Like?

One winter's day, shortly after Valentine's Day, Shawna received what could be considered her largest single-item donation:

13,000 heart-shaped lollipops. She was visiting a local food bank that shares donations with *Shawna's Outreach* and a pallet of lollipops had been donated. Shawna always likes to include a sweet treat in her outreach bags, so the food bank manager asked her if she would like some lollipops. The conversation went something like this:

"How many would you like?"

"I'll take whatever you can spare."

They started loading boxes into the trunk of Shawna's car, but they soon ran out of room. Since the lollipops were individually wrapped, Shawna suggested they empty the boxes directly into her trunk to save space. Before she knew it, her trunk had been filled with 13,000 lollipops!

Given the astonishing number of them, the sweet treats were distributed directly as part of the outreach bags given to homeless people, and then shared with multiple other worthy recipients. They went to:

- 1 fire department
- 4 street outreach organizations
- 1 women's outreach organization
- 2 community kitchens
- 1 food bank
- 1 men's shelter
- 4 retail stores (who like to spread cheer in their communities)

- 1 construction site (where workers were beyond excited to have a treat!)
- Several individuals who appreciated the pick-me-up or were happy to pass them on

This windfall resulted in many, many smiles and a lot of happy people who were touched by the simple gift of a strawberry-flavoured, heart-shaped lollipop.

Collaboration and Connection

Shawna's Outreach works with Ottawa charities in various ways. If Shawna doesn't think she can use a donation, she will direct it to another organization who may have a use for it. As a result, Shawna rarely refuses donations outright. Before accepting an item, if she knows she cannot use it for any reason or she is unable to store it, she will suggest an alternative recipient to her donors.

High Jinx—also known as Neighbours Helping Neighbours—is another grassroots initiative in Ottawa. Shawna regularly gives donations of frozen food to High Jinx for their community food pantry. She also directs those in need of food to organizations like High Jinx.

During the pandemic-imposed lock-downs, Morning Owl (a downtown coffee shop) repurposed their inside space to support a mini food bank. Since they were not allowed to offer dine-in service, they allowed *Shawna's Outreach* to use their space to collect food items. People in need signed up, and Shawna organized deliveries of this food to them.

Helping with Furniture has long been a designated drop-off location where donations for *Shawna's Outreach* can be left. The organization also helps promote Shawna's work through their own social media channels.

In the early days of the pandemic, Shawna arranged Christmas hampers for people in need. Some of the volunteer donors used the hampers as a teachable moment for their children, involving them in buying the items for the families who would receive them. Volunteers helped deliver the hampers; they thanked Shawna for providing them with "a slice of normalcy", by getting them out of the house and interacting with others during a time when lockdowns were preventing them from their regular activities. Sadly, *Shawna's Outreach* could not continue with the Christmas hampers in 2022: too many people were signing up and there were not enough sponsors to meet their needs.

At a higher level, Shawna strives to support and enhance existing social programs. When people needing food reach out to her, she asks them to also submit a request to the City of Ottawa through the 3-1-1 system. While *Shawna's Outreach* will continue to fill the gaps in community support for people in need, the scope of needs that remain unmet must be communicated to officials.

Despite the examples of heartfelt and successful collaboration among *Shawna's Outreach* and various businesses and individuals, there are also instances of individuals and companies claiming to support homeless people, for example through social media, and yet not honouring those claims. *Shawna's Outreach* has experienced this more than once: they create posts about helping the unhoused, using it to look good on social media, but in the end, they never go through with the donation.

Who Benefits from *Shawna's Outreach*?

The bags that Shawna fills to distribute to people on the street are gender neutral, so they can be handed out to both men and women, be they cis or trans. She no longer distributes feminine hygiene products because many of the women living on the street no longer require these products, due either to their living situation or their stage in life (post-menopausal), and some pharmacies and shelters provide feminine hygiene products to homeless women free of charge.

Shawna's outreach bags include a drink (juice/sports drink/water), a source of protein (bar/drink/meat), socks, and a cup of fruit/applesauce/pudding. When supplies permit, she also puts in candy/chocolate, toiletries, prepackaged snacks, hand sanitizer, mini towels, and a gift card. As of publication, Shawna has distributed 3,797 outreach bags to people in need. Shawna says, "These are full bags of supplies that cost me nothing—100 percent of the contents have been donated. Donors should be proud of the packages they helped put together. The contents of each bag, were someone to buy the items, would average $25 to $40. That's a huge accomplishment made possible by people working together and each one doing what they can."

Shawna has also shared hundreds of pounds of food that's been donated by a multitude of organizations. *Shawna's Outreach* never refuses any food donations. Homemade baked goods are by far the most popular donation for those on the receiving end. It is common for high school students to earn volunteer hours by baking goods for Shawna to hand out, and she is always happy to sign off on the requisite forms. Many homeless people have told Shawna that getting an outreach bag from her feels like opening a stocking on Christmas morning.

Shawna has helped people from all walks of life, including adults and children of all ages. While the majority of her recipients are teenagers and adults, she has also provided food to a child visiting their unhoused parent on the street. Older women, some not used to being helped, often put hand to heart and have tears in their eyes as they thank Shawna. She has heard, repeatedly, how they appreciate her looking them in the eye when they meet.

Shawna is known on the streets as "one of the good ones." A homeless man once introduced himself to her and told her, "Some days, you are the difference between life and death. And today is one of those days." Shawna went home feeling happy and sad: sad because of the ongoing needs on the streets, but more happy than sad because she recognizes the difference she is making and that she has others supporting *Shawna's Outreach*, since she acknowledges that she cannot do it alone.

In Shawna's experience, nobody that she has encountered on the street takes more than they need. In practical terms, they do not want to carry anything extra. At one time, a friend of Shawna's tried to give a panhandler a twenty-dollar bill, but he refused it. He indicated that five dollars would be plenty, and he did not want to take more than what he needed at that moment. If someone refuses an item she is offering with the words, "Give it to someone who needs it," Shawna will respond, "In this moment, nobody in the world needs what I am offering you more than you do. If you want it, it's yours."

When Shawna is distributing food, she sometimes has people ask for a little more: another bag of chips or a second chocolate bar. If she can spare the extra item, she will honour these requests. But if she has a line of people waiting for food, she will ask them to wait until everyone has had a chance to receive their first offering.

A Day in the Life of a Donation

Let's meet Hotel Hank, the complimentary bar of soap we all pick up on overnight hotel stays. His journey is one example of how even the smallest item can have a profound influence on someone's life.

Hotel Hank has been languishing on the stairs of a suburban Ottawa home for *at least* six months. Don't let his diminutive appearance fool you: he has big dreams. All he wants is to meet up with his pal, Water, and help someone get clean. Never quite making it to a water source, his mission has been thwarted. Until today.

9:37 a.m. A careless footfall on the stairs sends Hotel Hank reeling, tumbling end over end until he lands at the bottom of the stairs, slightly askew. The person responsible for said relocation picks up Hotel Hank with one hand, as the other hand scrolls distractedly on a smartphone.

9:38 a.m. A friend's social media post about *Shawna's Outreach* fills the smartphone screen. Coincidentally, it's a post detailing the need for toiletries.

9:39 a.m. Eyes shift from one hand to the other, from looking at Hotel Hank to reading the post about *Shawna's Outreach*. A lightbulb goes off as a plan is formed.

9:40 a.m. A direct message arrives at *Shawna's Outreach*: "Hi, I have a bar of soap that I'd like to donate. How can I get it to you?"

10:37 a.m. Hotel Hank is delivered to a local shop that serves as a drop-off point for *Shawna's Outreach*. Shawna will be coming by in a few hours to gather the items in this donation bin. In the meantime, Hotel Hank chills with the other products that are awaiting delivery to their final destination.

12:44 p.m. Shawna arrives and collects Hotel Hank and the other donated items. She brings them to the back of her vehicle and begins distributing them in the half-filled bags. Hotel Hank joins a bag that already contains the usual items (drink, source of protein, socks, etc.).

3:00 p.m. After a few additional stops to pick up more donations and sort them into waiting bags, Shawna arrives in downtown Ottawa to begin sharing the bags with the unhoused people she meets on the street.

4:12 p.m. The bag containing Hotel Hank is handed to a young man sitting on the curb. He quickly opens the bag and begins pulling out the items. A smile forms across his face as he takes out Hotel Hank, and he tells Shawna that he hasn't had a shower in four days. He's looking forward to using his new bar of soap—Hotel Hank.

5:13 p.m. Hotel Hank's dream comes true at last as he meets his pal, Water. More exuberant than soapy bubbles is his pride in helping this young homeless person. It's been a good day all around.

Chapter Three:
Challenges and Opportunities

The Challenge of Indifference

There are many challenges that accompany street outreach by kind souls like Shawna, and equally as many challenges that accompany homelessness. However, the biggest impediment that Shawna wants to highlight is the unfortunate absence of empathy among some residents. Shawna has witnessed it first-hand, both in people criticizing her good deeds and verbally pestering the unhoused. She has also heard countless stories from all corners; several examples are highlighted below.

There are many people who do not support the work that Shawna does or her approach to utilizing social media to raise awareness. Shawna has some friends, and even some family members, who scorn her choice to help homeless people in her adopted hometown. She's received messages telling her that she's promoting "poverty porn"—an emotion-provoking media tactic employed by some that exploits vulnerable people to increase donations. Sometimes individuals approach Shawna on the street, questioning what she is giving and to whom.

Shawna has both witnessed and heard stories of people yelling at panhandlers, asking, for example, "Why don't you just get a job?" Instead of yelling back at them, Shawna tries to engage them in thoughtful conversation. She'll ask them about the intricacies of job hunting: "What's the first thing you need when you apply for a job? You need contact information for follow-up: an address and a telephone number. People living on the streets or those staying at a shelter who fill in their social worker's information on a job application are unlikely to hear back from a prospective employer. And if a homeless person walks into a business to apply for a job, not having washed recently or wearing stained or ripped clothing, it's very unlikely that they will be asked back for an interview."

Educated, unhoused people face other challenges beyond unemployment. The social workers, who are working diligently to help these individuals find paid employment and housing, are overworked and understaffed. Add to that a lack of affordable housing, and the cards are stacked against homeless people who are trying to get back on their feet. They face challenge, after challenge, after challenge. While it's true, of course, that people living in stable housing suffer misfortune from time to time, adversities are amplified for those living on the street.

Shawna has also been told that anything she gives to an unhoused person will subsequently be traded for crack or another illicit drug. Realistically, a muffin and a banana won't amount to payment for crack.

On one occasion, a man confronted Shawna and asked why she was giving a sandwich to a homeless woman lying in an expensive sleeping bag. What he didn't understand is that Shawna redistributes whatever goods are donated to her, and this unhoused person did not choose the pricy sleeping bag. She would have been grateful for any warm covering for sleeping outside. Shawna has also received high-end clothing from a local consignment shop and has given those items to people on the street. Her philosophy is: "I give what I get," whatever that amounts to. On occasion, donors have advised Shawna on who should be given their items, for example, "Someone deserving," "Someone who looks normal," or "Someone who's clean." Shawna doesn't want any conditions on donations. If a donor wishes to specify where their donations should go, she recommends that they give to an organization that is equipped to handle directed donations. She doesn't have time to explain where each banana or pair of socks or scarf will go.

When Shawna takes the time to respond to those who criticize her acts of kindness, she never confronts them; instead, she tries to educate them in the hope that they will develop empathy for those less fortunate than themselves. Some thank her for her time and appreciate the lessons they have learned. Others simply roll their eyes, presumably thinking they "know better." Nevertheless, Shawna tries to convince people to help; "If that negative energy could be channeled into something positive, imagine the changes we could make."

The Challenge of Street Violence

Unhoused people, just like those who have stable housing, crave kindness, but violence is ever-present on the streets. Many homeless people have been spat on, kicked, or bullied. Some feel safer sleeping outside than within a shelter, even though a night on the street in the winter could lead to frostbite or even freezing to death. Unfortunately, violence is a daily threat on the street.

Early on in Shawna's outreach work, she visited a homeless encampment. Shawna asked for, and was granted by the people who stayed there, permission to enter this space. She was welcomed back when she returned regularly with blankets, food, and other items. Sadly, living in this encampment wasn't safer than living on the street. When the media spread reports about the encampment, outsiders showed up on multiple nights to threaten and, in some cases, injure those in the tents. The intruders beat at the tents with hammers and metal rods in an effort to force the people inside to flee. Eventually, an agreement was reached between people staying there and city officials, and the tented area was removed peacefully by city officials.

While the majority of unhoused people appreciate all that Shawna does for them, there are some people on the street who may not want help. It is rare, but outreach workers have faced violence from homeless people. Shawna has learned the safest times of the day and month to deliver her outreach bags.

The Challenge of Furry Friends and Life on the Street

Some homeless people have their pets living with them on the street. In many cases, they had their pets before they became unhoused, while in other cases, they may have "adopted" stray or orphaned animals later on. Pets provide companionship, security, warmth, and love. Who among us would reject a beloved pet if we found ourselves homeless?

Some people who pan with their pets are given dog food, first and foremost. While the pet owners are grateful, it's a sad reality that humans will help animals above their fellow humans. This is yet another way in which homeless people are being given the message that they are worthless. When this message is constant, it becomes internalized and hard to disbelieve. In contrast, their furry friends are a source of unconditional love, providing what's often lacking in their human interactions.

The Opportunity to Raise Awareness

A question for Shawna: "What do you want people to take away from this book?"

Shawna's answer: "Awareness. Awareness about the 'system' that is set up to help those in need. While it's true that the system is set up to help, there is no guarantee that individuals in need will be able to access this help. Awareness about the challenges of navigating health care, housing, pharmacare, food and water, child care, and schooling. Many Canadians assume that the support will flow if they need it, but that's not necessarily the case. The barriers and restrictions that exist in every aspect of the Canadian social safety net mean that its services are not always accessible for those in need, particularly for low- or no-income

Canadians." Shawna has experienced first-hand the organizations that exist to support people in need; she has seen what is lacking in the system and how easily people can fall through the cracks of our social safety net. This is why she helps where and how she can: with kindness and a bite to eat.

Shawna's goal is to broaden awareness of the needs of vulnerable people and inspire us to truly see the unhoused without judgement. She encourages us all to investigate the social services that are available, find out where the gaps are, and help fill those gaps by getting help to people who need it.

The Opportunity to Help

These are Shawna's recommendations on how you can help:

- Visit the Facebook page for *Shawna's Outreach* to see the regularly updated list of needed items. [More details are available in the Appendix.]
- Contact any of your elected officials (municipal, provincial, and/or federal) about the housing crisis or other factors that negatively impact the unhoused population.

- Contact a local shelter and volunteer your time.
- Research the root cause of the growing homelessness crisis and how you could help enact change.
- Donate time, food, or funds to your local food bank.
- Donate to places that make you feel good.
- Help when you can.
- Share positivity. Be kind.

If you aren't in a position to donate, that's okay. There is no judgement for people who can't give.

If you don't agree with what Shawna does, she can live with that. If you prefer to donate to another charity, she applauds your generosity. Shawna does not judge others, nor how or who they help. She says, "Whatever speaks to you, put your energy into helping there."

When Helping is Free

Helping doesn't have to cost money! It can include intangibles like online communication: sharing a social media post or giving it a "like" to help boost its online reach. Shawna has observed that some unhoused and vulnerable people who follow her social media page are the ones who most often click "like" and share her posts. They are giving, even though they don't have tangible items to donate and are often on the receiving end of Shawna's donations. To which Shawna says, "That is just awesome. It reinforces my mantra that when we each give a little, a lot gets done."

Word of mouth is a powerful—and free—way to help. When individuals tell friends and family about people in need and what's being done to help them, it increases exposure for *Shawna's Outreach* or other charitable initiatives. Teaching children about the importance of helping those less fortunate and showing them empathy is an untapped opportunity to help. Many of the people Shawna speaks to on the street say they wish people would acknowledge them with eye contact and maybe even a smile, instead of looking through them: "See me, I'm here. You don't have to help me with money, but you can help me with hope."

Shawna regularly receives messages such as, "Hey, I just heard about what you do, and I love it. How can I help?" It is the power of communication that helps get the word out and allows Shawna to continue *Shawna's Outreach*. However, many people say, "If ever you need something, let me know." This type of offer is challenging, because Shawna does not have the time or energy to chase people down for possible donations that most often never appear. If someone wants to donate, they can.

Shawna is always looking for new places where she can offer donations that cannot be distributed through her outreach: "The more places we know about, the more people we may be able to help." We can also share items efficiently and with people who can use them.

If you live outside Ottawa, Shawna encourages you to learn about the needs of homeless people in your own town or city and opportunities for helping them. For example, Shawna recommends that if you work in a restaurant or bakery, find out how you can donate leftovers. The same applies if you find yourself in a meeting or at an event that has ordered too much food for participants—with a bit of effort, that food can be redirected to hungry people.

Safety and Respect, First and Foremost

If you are inclined to directly support unhoused people, Shawna has some tips for you:

When approaching people on the street, maintain an arm's-length distance. Even inadvertently, someone could injure you with a needle or other sharp object in their possession.

Be patient and polite. These are vulnerable people who do not yet know if they can trust you, and they may have experienced violence at the hands of strangers in the past. It may take time to gain their trust.

Announce yourself in a non-threatening way. Shawna's standard opening is: "Hi friends. I have outreach supplies if you need or want anything."

Look at the people you intend to help; look them in the eye so they know they have your attention.

If you offer help to someone on the street and they say, "No," respect their decision. No always means No. They may not be able to carry it. If food has been offered and refused, they may have already eaten, have food allergies or dislikes. Do not judge or criticize them as being ungrateful if they refuse your offer.

Do not trade food or donations for photos or social media posts. Respect the privacy of all those you meet.

Appendix

Shawna's Wish List

Shawna's Outreach maintains a Facebook page because there is no cost associated with it. On that page, Shawna regularly shares a wish list of supplies that are in urgent need, as well as an Amazon wish list for those who don't have stuff to give but still want to help. Shawna wants everyone to know that food is always accepted; if she cannot store it safely (e.g., frozen items), she will redistribute it to other charitable organizations. Undergarments such as long johns, socks, and new underwear can always be donated. And gift cards for food establishments, grocery stores, and pharmacies will never be refused.

These lists change depending on the season and current inventory. Please visit *Shawna's Outreach – Ottawa* (https://www.facebook.com/

<u>profile.php?id=100077647275648</u>) to see if the current wish list (as of the time of publication) has been updated.

Facebook List

Items include:
- Food: non-perishable and individually wrapped, e.g.,
    - cookies, crackers, meal replacement bars, juice, fruit snacks, etc.
- Clothing:
    - outerwear, such as hats, rain gear, thermal blankets, etc.
    - personal items, such as socks, underwear, etc.
- Toiletries: travel-size, e.g.,
    - soap, shampoo, conditioner, lotion, wipes, toothpaste, mouthwash, etc.
- Gift cards for:
    - restaurants
    - grocery stores
    - pharmacies

Amazon List

Want to help but don't live in the Ottawa area? Can't get out to shop? Can't drop off? The Amazon wish list is available! The list of items is continually adjusted to match current needs. When you order an item from the list, it ships directly to Shawna's door. You can also access a link to this wish list via the Facebook page for *Shawna's Outreach* (https://www.amazon.ca/hz/wishlist/ls/2RD9MRDNTILAX?ref_=wl_share&fbclid=IwAR1jmYGDdQGl4zzyDSomnHJkPaxnY_wiJXCC0ksl3qunCsBFnlc74lDBq-Y).

Direct Donations

If you would like to donate directly to Shawna's Outreach, you can email shawnasoutreach@gmail.com.

Glossary of Terms

Charitable organization: Also known as a charity or nonprofit organization. A type of organization that operates for the public benefit and exists to address specific social, cultural, or environmental issues. Charitable organizations are typically established to provide services, support a cause, or undertake activities that improve the well-being of individuals or communities. They are governed by specific legal regulations and must meet certain criteria to qualify for tax-exempt status.

Grassroots initiative: A volunteer-led movement or project that originates at the local level. Grassroots initiatives typically do not receive funding from governments and have no official charitable status.

Homeless/Unhoused: People that currently do not have a permanent residence and hence are forced to live on the streets or within temporary shelters. Also can be kindly referred to as Unsheltered.

Outreach/outreach walk: Outings to find vulnerable people who are living on the streets, and offering support that they may need. It can include: directions to services such as first aid, food banks, or mental health support; or transportation to essential services. Outreach workers also carry commonly needed supplies with them to distribute, such as blankets, clothing, food, and other provisions.

Panning: Also known as panhandling. The act of seeking loose change or small donations from individuals or passersby. Homeless people who panhandle often do so as a means of obtaining immediate financial assistance to meet their basic needs, such as food, shelter, or other essential items.

Poverty porn: A media tactic that exploits vulnerable people to increase donations by using emotion-triggering imagery.

Social enterprise: An organization or business that combines entrepreneurial principles with a social or environmental mission. Social enterprises typically generate revenue through their operations, which they reinvest into their social mission or use to create a positive social impact.

Vulnerable people: People who have no or low incomes; who may have suffered abuse, trauma or oppression; who may also be unhoused; and are in need of support.

Acknowledgements

The editorial team donated their time and services for free. As a result, all of the royalties earned from the sale of this book will go directly to *Shawna's Outreach*.

> Editing: Christie Phillips
> (surfwpb@gmail.com) and
> Jennifer Rae-Brown
> (raebrownjennifer@gmail.com)
> Layout: Matthew Bin
> (mattbin@gmail.com)
> Writing: Amanda Sterczyk
> (sterczyk@gmail.com)

The following organizations and individuals accept donations for *Shawna's Outreach* (current at time of printing):

> Helping With Furniture, 1455
> Michael St, Unit 3, Ottawa,
> Ontario
> (https://www.hwfottawa.org/)

> Morning Owl Coffeehouse & Parlour, 229 Armstrong St, Ottawa, Ontario (https://morningowl.ca/)
> The Twisted Fork, Perth, Ontario (https://www.facebook.com/twistedforkcafe/)
> Cathy Greely, Ontario
> Monique (M² Cleaning Ottawa), Orleans, Ontario (https://m2cleaningottawa.ca/)
> Patrick, Barrhaven, Ottawa, Ontario

The following individual and organizations gave permission to use their names:
> Tanya O'Connor: Project Purse, Tampon Tuesday, Project Winter Warmth
> Helping with Furniture
> High Jinx
> Morning Owl Coffeehouse & Parlour
> Revel Academy

About the Authors

Shawna Thibodeau is a passionate Maritimer driven by her own experiences with hunger, abuse, and navigating the difficult "systems". She who, without judgement, recognizes the challenges of vulnerable people and selflessly dedicates her time to help them, while also taking care of her family. Connect with Shawna via email: shawnasoutreach@gmail.com.

Amanda Sterczyk, an international author, has consistently been a fervent advocate of aiding those in need. Connect with Amanda by visiting her website: amandasterczyk.com.

www.ingramcontent.com/pod-product-compliance
Lightning Source LLC
Chambersburg PA
CBHW051844250726

48659CB00005B/2005